# The Old Promise

Written by
**Rob Waring** and **Maurice Jamall**
(with contributions by **Julian Thomlinson**)

D0584517

# Before You Read

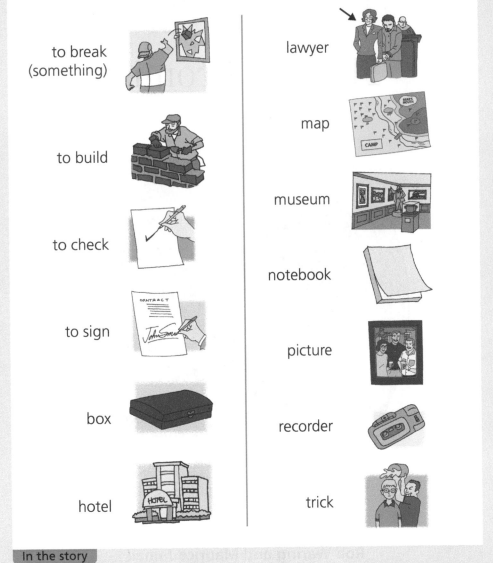

to break (something)

to build

to check

to sign

box

hotel

lawyer

map

museum

notebook

picture

recorder

trick

Faye    John    Tyler    Mr. Jenkins    Mr. Walsh    Mrs. Dale

"Do you understand now?" asked Faye.

"Yes, I think so," replied Ryan.

Faye was helping Ryan Walsh at his house. She often came and helped Ryan with his homework. Faye and Ryan finished their work and Faye decided to go home.

"Good," she said. "I'll go home now. See you at school tomorrow."

When Faye was putting her papers in her bag, she saw some old things on the table. There were some old pens, and some old papers. "What are these old things?" she asked Ryan.

"Oh those?" he replied. "They're my father's. He likes making things."

Faye said, "Oh, I see. I'm going now. I'll see you at school tomorrow."

"Thanks, Faye," Ryan said. "You're a big help."

Faye replied, "You're welcome."

Faye and Ryan walked to the front door. "Okay, see you later," she said.

Just then, Don Walsh, Ryan's father, came out of a room. He was walking very quickly to the front door. He was holding many papers and a red box. He was not looking where he was going. He pushed the door open and it hit Faye and she fell down. Mr. Walsh's papers went everywhere.

"Ouch," said Faye.

Mr. Walsh said, "Be careful, girl! Look where you're going!"
He was angry with her.

"Oh, I'm sorry!" said Faye.

Faye helped pick up the papers. She saw some old papers.
Mr. Walsh took the papers from her very quickly. "Those are
my papers," he said angrily. "They're mine and very
important." He put the papers in the red box. Faye was very
surprised.

"Oh, I'm sorry, Mr. Walsh," she said.

Faye went to see her friends, John and Tyler. Tyler said, "Hi, Faye. Mr. Jenkins just called." Mr. Jenkins was their friend. He was a kind old man who lived in a big old house on the hill.

"Oh, really?" said Faye. "Why?"

John replied, "We don't know. He said he wants us to see him soon."

Faye replied, "Okay, let's go and see him."

Faye, John, and Tyler went to Mr. Jenkins's house. Mr. Walsh was there, too. He was talking to Mr. Jenkins. "You have to give me the house," he said.

Mr. Jenkins was looking at an old piece of paper. "But I don't want to leave this house. This is my home," he said.

"You must leave. You read the paper. You know what it says," said Mr. Walsh.

He continued, "I'll be back at 4 o'clock. You can sign the papers then." He walked out of the door.

Just then Faye came in. Mr. Walsh nearly hit Faye. "You again!" he said angrily. "Be careful, girl! Look where you're going!"

Tyler, John, and Faye went in the house. Faye thought, "I don't like that man!"

"Oh, hello everybody," Mr. Jenkins said slowly. He was usually very happy to see them, but today he looked very sad.

"Are you okay?" John asked Mr. Jenkins. "You don't look very well."

Mr. Jenkins looked at the drink in front of him, but he did not drink it. He was holding the piece of paper. He read it again. He read it many times. But it was always the same.

"What's wrong, Mr. Jenkins?" they asked. "What happened?"

"Sit down," said Mr. Jenkins. "I have some bad news. It's this paper." They sat down around the table, listening carefully.

Mr. Jenkins said slowly, "This paper says that 100 years ago my grandfather agreed with Mr. Walsh's grandfather that the Jenkins family could live here for 100 years. But they agreed that after 100 years, my family must give back the house to the Walsh family. Today is the last day. I must now leave this house."

"What?" said John.

"Yes. That's right. I have to leave this house, my home," said Mr. Jenkins. He looked so sad. "What am I going to do now? I don't want to go, but I have to."

Tyler said, "You should call your lawyer and check the paper. You should check if it's real."

"Yes, that's a good idea," Mr. Jenkins said. "Thanks."

Mr. Jenkins called his family lawyer, Mrs. Dale. Soon she came to the house.

"Mr. Jenkins, what's this bad news?" she asked.

"Do you know Don Walsh?" he asked.

"No, not at all," she replied. "Why? Who's Don Walsh?"

Mr. Jenkins replied, "He gave me this paper. It says I have to give this house to him." He showed her the paper. It looked very old.

"What?" she said. She was very surprised.

She read it, and looked at it for a long time. Then she looked up and said sadly, "I'm sorry, Mr. Jenkins. This paper says you must leave this house."

"Oh no," he said.

"I'm sorry, Mr. Jenkins," she said. "It's so sad because you were born here."

Tyler asked, "Why does Mr. Walsh want the house?"

"I guess he wants to live here," replied Mr. Jenkins.

Faye was very surprised. "But he has a big new home. This house is old. I don't understand. Why does he want to live here? You'd get only a little money if you sold this house."

Mrs. Dale said, "Yes, that is strange, isn't it?"
She continued, "Mr. Jenkins, maybe I can help. This paper looks very old. But you should check if it's real."
"Of course, but how do I do that?" he asked.
"Take it to Bayview Museum, and ask them to check if it's old," she said.
Tyler said, "That's a great idea. We should go now. Mr. Walsh is coming here at 4 o'clock."
Then Faye asked, "Can I look at the paper please?" Mrs. Dale gave her the paper.
Faye looked at it and said, "Hmm." She was thinking.

Suddenly, she turned to John and said, "John, come with me, I need your help."

"My help?" said John. "Umm . . . How? How can I help?"

Faye replied, "There's no time for questions, John. I have an idea. Come on. Hurry, we have to go now."

She said to Tyler and Mr. Jenkins, "John and I are going now, we'll see you later."

"Come on," she said to John. "We have to hurry. There isn't much time."

Faye and John ran out of the house. "Where are we going, Faye?" he asked.

"To Mr. Walsh's house," she replied. John just looked at her. He did not understand.

Faye continued, "That paper looked strange. There's something wrong with it."

John replied, "What's wrong with it?"

"I don't know now. We're going to find out," she said. "And I think I know Mrs. Dale, too. But I can't remember where I saw her."

When they got to Mr. Walsh's house, nobody was home. Faye said, "John, help me. Find something to break the window."

"What?" said John. "You want me to break the window?"

"Of course!" she replied. "Nobody's home. We can't get in. There's something inside the house I want to see. We have to break a window. Hurry."

John gave Faye a stone. "Thanks. Is anybody looking?" asked Faye. John looked around and replied, "No. I don't think so."

"Good," she said.

Mrs. Dale, Mr. Jenkins, and Tyler went to Bayview Museum. There, they met Mr. Harding.

"Hello, I'm Kevin Harding," he said to Mrs. Dale. "How can I help you?"

"It's nice to meet you, Mr. Harding. I'm Margaret Dale," she said. "We need you to look at this paper. How old is it?" she asked.

Mr. Jenkins gave the paper to Mr. Harding. "I don't know. I'll have to look at it."

Mr. Harding looked at the paper for a long time. "Hmm, I think the paper is about 80 to 100 years old," he said.

Mr. Jenkins asked, "So, is the paper real?"

"Yes, it is," replied Mr. Harding. "It's very old."

"Oh, that's terrible, Mr. Jenkins," said Mrs. Dale. "I'm so sorry for you."

Mr. Jenkins was very sad. "Now I *have to* leave my house," he thought.

Mrs. Dale said, "I'm sorry, but we must get back to the house. Mr. Walsh is coming at 4 o'clock."

Faye and John went into Mr. Walsh's house through the window. Faye was looking for something.

John was very worried. "Faye, we'll be in a lot of trouble if they come back," he said.

"I know," she said. "So hurry and help me find them."

"What are we looking for?" asked John.

"Some papers. I saw Mr. Walsh put them in a red box," she replied. Then she saw it. "Ah, there's the box. It's on his table."

Faye looked at the papers and said, "I was right!" She smiled. John was surprised, "Faye. I don't understand. What are you talking about?"

"Look at these papers?" Faye said. "They are the same as the one Mr. Walsh gave Mr. Jenkins!" She showed him the papers. "But the paper Mr. Walsh gave Mr. Jenkins isn't old," said John.

"No, the *paper* is old!" she said. "But Mr. Walsh wrote it! He used old paper. His grandfather didn't write it."

"But why?" asked John.

"Because," she said, "Mr. Walsh wants to trick Mr. Jenkins. He wants Mr. Jenkins to give him his house." John could not believe it.

Just then, Faye saw a notebook on the table. She picked it up and looked at it carefully. She picked up a pencil and started to write.
"There's no time for writing, Faye," he said. "They will come home soon and catch us."
But Faye did not answer. She just looked at the notebook.
"Wow!" she said. "We need this, too."
"Faye, you're very strange," said John. Then he saw a picture on the table.
"Look at this picture!" he said excitedly. He showed it to Faye and smiled.
"Great! Bring that, too," she said.

They ran out of the house. Faye said, "Come on, John. We have to hurry. Mr. Walsh is coming at 4 o'clock."

"No," said John. He stopped running. "You go, Faye. I have a plan."

"What plan?" asked Faye.

"It's okay, I know a way to stop Mr. Walsh," he said. "I'll meet you at Mr. Jenkins's house."

Faye replied, "No, I'll come with you! What's your idea?"

22

It was 4 o'clock. Mr. Walsh was at Mr. Jenkins's house.
Mrs. Dale spoke to Mr. Walsh.

"Mr. Walsh. I'm Margaret Dale. I'm Mr. Jenkins's lawyer,"
she said.

"Is everything okay with the paper?" Mr. Walsh asked.

"There is nothing wrong with it," she said. "We took the
paper to the museum. The man there checked the paper
and said it's old. But Mr. Walsh, please think again. Mr.
Jenkins doesn't want to leave. This is his home. Please
don't ask him to give back the house."

"I see. Thank you, Mrs. Dale," said Mr. Walsh, smiling.

"I'm sorry, but the house is mine. And I want it back."

Mr. Walsh looked at Mr. Jenkins. He said, "Mr. Jenkins, I have the papers for you. You have to sign them. Your lawyer agrees the paper is real." He pointed at the papers on the table.

"I don't want to sign," he said. "I don't want to leave. Mrs. Dale, do I have to sign?"

"I'm sorry, Mr. Jenkins," said his lawyer. "The paper looks okay, but I want Mr. Walsh to think again about this."

"No, I'm sorry," he said. "Your grandfather made a promise and you must keep it."

Tyler watched Mr. Jenkins pick up a pen. "Oh, no," he thought. "He has to leave his home."

Just then, Faye and John ran into the room.

Faye had a book in her hand. She saw Mr. Jenkins with the pen in his hand. "Stop! Don't sign that! I have some great news, Mr. Jenkins," said Faye. Everybody looked at her.

"Mr. Jenkins, you do not have to leave here! You can stay here!" she continued.

Faye turned to Mr. Walsh, and said, "Mr. Walsh I know your plan. You don't want to live here. You want Mr. Jenkins's house because you want to build a big hotel here."

"That's not right," said Mr. Walsh.

"Yes, it is. Mr. Jenkins, look at this." She showed Mr. Jenkins the notebook.

She put the book on the table. She got a pencil. She started writing. "You can see where the pencil was," she said. "If you write over it gently, then you can see the writing under it. See!"

She showed the paper to Mr. Jenkins. She read it to everybody. "New Hotel plan, 175 rooms, for Jenkins Bay Hotel, building starts next month," she read.

"But, Faye," asked Tyler. "How did you know about the hotel? How did you get the paper?"

She replied, "John and I went to Mr. Walsh's house and found this paper on his table."

"Wow! That's smart, Faye," Tyler said.

Mr. Walsh was very angry. "You went into my house?"

But Mr. Jenkins was angrier. He said, "So, Mr. Walsh, you lied to me. You don't want to live here. You want to build a hotel!"

"Okay, so I want to build a hotel. But you have to give me the house," said Mr. Walsh angrily. "The paper says so. Your lawyer says so. It's my house now."

"No, the paper's not real," said John. "We found these."
He showed some papers to everybody.
Mr. Jenkins looked at them. "These are the same as the
paper Mr. Walsh gave me," he said.
"Yes," said John. "Mr. Walsh wrote that paper. The paper
is old, but the writing is not. He wrote it a few days ago."
Mrs. Dale said, "But the man in the museum . . . he said it
was old."
Faye said, "He was talking about the paper, not about
the writing." Everybody looked at Faye.
"And we know why he lied," said John.

Faye asked Mrs. Dale, "Mrs. Dale, do you know Mr. Walsh, or Mr. Harding?"

"No, we met today. Why do you ask?" asked Mrs. Dale.

"I see," replied Faye. Then she asked, "Mr. Walsh, do you know Mrs. Dale, or Mr. Harding?"

Mr. Walsh replied, "No. I don't know them at all. Who's Mr. Harding?"

Faye turned to Mr. Jenkins and said, "They are lying. They made a plan to work together to take this house from you."

"What are you talking about, Faye?" said Mr. Jenkins. He was very shocked.

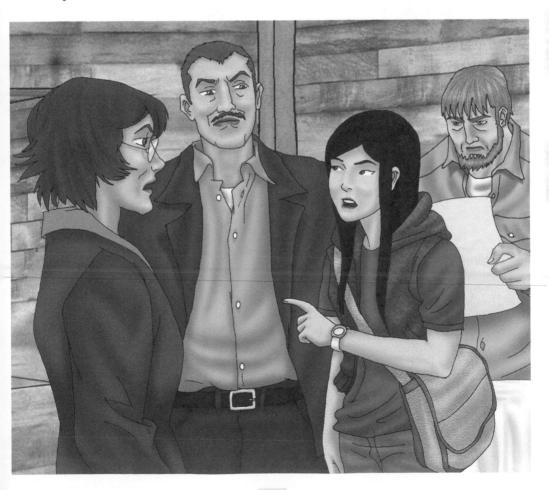

Faye showed them the picture from Mr. Walsh's table. It was an old picture of Mr. Harding, Mrs. Dale, and Mr. Walsh.

"See? They did not meet today. They lied," said Faye. "They are old friends. This picture shows us. They made a plan together to trick you."

"Why you . . . !" said Mr. Walsh. He was very angry. "Give me that picture!"

"No," said Faye. "The police need to see it."

Mr. Jenkins said, "Thank you, thank you, Faye and John."
"That's okay," said Faye. "We wanted to help."
Mr. Walsh looked at Mrs. Dale. They both understood. Their
plan did not work, so they decided to run away. Mr. Walsh and
Mrs. Dale ran to the door. Mr. Walsh opened the door.
"You'll never catch us," he said. "The police will never believe
you."
"Yes, they will," said John. He showed them a recorder under
his shirt. "The police heard everything."

The police were waiting outside.

John said to everybody, "The police know about the paper, and they know about their plans. I called the police and told them you were here."

The police officers caught Mrs. Dale and Mr. Walsh.

Tyler said to the police officer, "I think Mr. Harding at the museum is working with Mrs. Dale and Mr. Walsh."

"Thank you," said the police officer. "We'll go and talk to him."

Mr. Jenkins said, "Faye and John, thank you so much." He smiled. "Now I can stay here."